LIBRA HOROSCOPE
2015

Lisa Lazuli

Lisa Lazuli is the author of the amazon bestseller

HOROSCOPE 2014: ASTROLOGY and NUMEROLOGY HOROSCOPES

ABOUT THE AUTHOR

Lisa Lazuli studied astrology with the Faculty of Astrological Studies in London.

She has practiced since 1999.

Lisa has been a regular guest on BBWM and BBC Shropshire talking about astrology and doing both horoscopes and live readings. She has also made guest appearances on Fox FM, BBC Cambridgeshire, BBC Northamptonshire, BBC Coventry and Warwickshire and US Internet Radio Shows including the Debra Clement Show.

Lisa wrote horoscopes for Asian Woman Magazine.

Now available in eBook and paperback:

TAURUS: Your Day, Your Decan, Your Sign *The most REVEALING book on The Bull yet.* Includes 2015 Predictions.

ARIES HOROSCOPE 2015

TAURUS HOROSCOPE 2015

GEMINI HOROSCOPE 2015

CANCER HOROSCOPE 2015

LEO HOROSCOPE 2015

VIRGO HOROSCOPE 2015

Lisa Lazuli is also the author of

The mystery/thrillers:

A Sealed Fate

Holly Leaves

Next of Sin

As well as:

Delicious, Nutritious Recipes for the Time and Cash Strapped

Paleo Diet: Get Started, Get Motivated, Feel Great.

99 ACE Places to Promote Your Book

Pressure Cooking Reinvented.

FOREWARD

Dear Reader,

I hope my yearly horoscopes will provide you with some insightful guidance during what is a very tricky time astrologically speaking with the heavy planets i.e. Pluto and Uranus at loggerheads in cardinal signs and Neptune in Pisces calling us all to get in touch with our spiritual side.

I have a conversational style of writing, please excuse any grammatical errors, I write much as I would speak.

As the song goes, "Nobody said it was easy." I know the mass media pump-out shows us plenty about quick fix love, money, fame and success; however, life is a journey filled with challenges and obstacles designed to encourage us to find out what we are made of and who we really are.

Embrace the good and bad and enjoy what is your unique experience.

Be the hero in your own personal life movie and never hide your spotlight.

I must add that the best astrology insights are gained from a unique chart based on your time, date, year and place of birth.

If you would like your natal chart calculated for FREE, click here:

http://lisalazuli.com/2014/06/30/would-you-like-to-know-where-all-your-planets-are-free-natal-chart/

Please join me on Facebook:

https://www.facebook.com/pages/Lisa-Lazuli-Astrologer/192000594298158?ref=hl

Contents

Overview 9

JANUARY 2015 15

FEBRUARY 2015 19

MARCH 2015 23

APRIL 2015 27

MAY 2015 29

JUNE 2015 33

JULY 2015 35

AUGUST 2015 37

SEPTEMBER 2015 41

OCTOBER 2015 45

NOVEMBER 2015 49

DECEMBER 2015 53

This is a highly significant year during what is a significant and life-altering phase for Libra. Your core purpose and destiny seem aligned with both your ego and your spiritual will. So many times in life we drift along in a frustrating stalemate where our ego seems to be at odds with our true path and purpose in life, but when those two align, miracles are possible and positive thinking and mind power really work.

When we are young, we often have a yearning, something that nags at us, compelling us in a certain direction, but often we are confused as to what path it is we should be taking to truly express our beliefs, talents and core values. This year, things will click, and you will find it much easier to make choices that are true to you and which set you on a path where you feel a sense of purpose and destiny.

There is a large degree of good karma attached to 2015, with things you worked hard on and good deeds from the past paying off.

In life, we make decisions based on ego considerations, but those are often not decisions that are good for us and which reflect our true destiny. This is a year when your ego may get knocked back through circumstances, but where your spiritual will can shine through, showing to you a purpose in life and a destiny far greater that your ego ever dreamed of. "What is essential is invisible to the eye, only the heart can see rightly!"

Partnership and cooperation are vital this year to your self-development – it is also through the eyes of others, especially those close to you that you can gain a perspective on yourself. Librans are team players; this year will be a case in point, but it is you who must lead the team. Libra will be required to give both moral and strategic leadership; this is an opportunity to make noble decisions and navigate your team to a successful outcome. The challenge is to let yourself rely on others, to place your trust in them and to know who you can place that trust in.

You must guard against being excessively competitive and seeing winning as the only outcome of importance. Do not be hasty or rash or sacrifice personal happiness for issues that are not that important or fundamental. This is not a year to work in isolation; even if you do not work with others per se, you must look at the broader context of what you are doing and striving for – you must constantly look for feedback and even criticism, take what others say on board. Partnership and being able to see ourselves through the eyes of others is essential for balance and perspective.

The power in Pluto is still acting on Libra as it will for a few more years to come, and this brings both opportunity for growth, introspection and even radical life change. Pluto is not superficial; it gets right to the core of any matter compelling you to delve into your psyche to get in touch with your core purpose and to rediscover your personal power. We all give up our power as we go along in life: we allow ourselves to be controlled by money, by loved ones, by parents, by our fears, by government even. Sometimes, we get so bogged down by routine that we even forget we have any power at all. When Pluto is in hard aspect to the Sun, it can throw many spanners in the works of our lives and while these can be perceived as a threat and a traumatic experience, Pluto is trying to break up the routines and structure of our lives to waken us to new possibilities and to encourage us to dig deep and rediscover the hero inside of ourselves. Pluto is giving you the chance to regenerate and rejuvenate your life by letting go of false attachments that are not contributing to your growth, and which in some cases are only entrapping you in a cycle or loop that is going nowhere.

Endings and beginnings this year hold the prospect of long-term opportunity and can inject your life with a fulfillment or purpose that was either lacking or unclear. Not everything in life can be imbued with meaning, but this year one must certainly watch closely and attach a meaning and a higher purpose to events.

Self-honesty and self-awareness are demanded this year, and that can require maturity – be willing to learn about yourself, even if what you learn surprises you. Relationships are key to self-understanding this year as it is within close encounters that deep emotional and psychological complexes emerge and can be tackled. Pluto is all about shining light into dark places, revealing and understanding what is hidden or even taboo. This is your opportunity to accept, transform or confront your issues.

You have the strong desire in 2015 to look beneath the surface and to go beyond the obvious – your investigative yearning is strong as is your desire to get to the truth. You are highly critical in your thinking and able to gain a penetrative insight into information. This can be very helpful in interpersonal communications and within careers where you must analyze data and then act on it.

You are fascinated by secrets and mysteries, and that interest may range from neighborhood intrigue to international intrigue and conspiracy theories. It is your desire to get at the whole truth that will compel you to take a long look at all the details – you are not interested in what is superficial this year, but in what is real, even if what is real is uncomfortable to hear.

This is a highly imaginative and creative year – Librans involved in the arts, music, film and fashion can take advantage of being highly inspired and creative. Librans in non-arts professions may find relaxation and escapism in art or music as a hobby.

Librans are known to be very fair-minded and rational. However, this year your passions and emotions can erupt from nowhere and cloud your judgment at times – reason and logic can be cast aside in an irrational or even paranoid outburst. Emotions and issues you have buried and hidden for many a year may suddenly insist on expression via the out of character outbursts. The key is more self-honesty. Librans are people pleasers, who need harmony and peaceful relations to function at their best; this, however, leads you to sweep certain emotions under the carpet as you feel they are not compatible with your nature. This year you need to acknowledge and own all your emotions, and that means not suppressing gut reactions to places and people. Follow your instinct more, even if it defies the logic and rationale you usually rely on.

Your sense of humor is excellent this year, you are very witty and quite ironic – you can extract the humor from every situation. I think it is partly your penetrative insights into people and situations which aid your wit this year. Wit can also be a way you can deal with difficult emotional situations or even the way you can express something that may be hard to say directly.

A certain amount of secrecy and coyness is required this year – do not be an open book, keep parts of your life private, and pay more attention to how you can protect yourself.

Librans are known for their global view, you are seldom small-minded NIMBY's – this year you are sure to act with high moral and ethical standards in everything you do, and within your teams and groups you will expect the same from others. You can become quickly angered when you feel that those you care for do not have respect for the same high values as you do – you will do your best to change them. Change for the better is a theme for you in 2015, and you will work hard to change the world around you in a practical way, you won't just be talking about it round the fire, you are resolved to take action, and you can be highly effective. You really believe in what you are doing in 2015, and that is why your leadership is highly motivational and inspiring for others. If a call to action is to be made, it is you who can make it – you have the power to whip others up from their complacency to realize that they too can make a difference. In your community or within local politics take direct action and believe in yourself.

Librans are restless this year and keen for activities which inspire them and which have meaning; you are also keen to inspire others – perhaps politically, perhaps about health. We have talked about inspiring others to stand up and be counted in politics via local action groups, maybe you will rather start a local running club to inspire others to become fitter or a cooking club to try new diet recipes; maybe you will raise awareness for a charity. The theme is taking action and not being complacent and motivating others, i.e. friends and family to join you in that action.

Librans are keen to change things around them this year, and that includes people – but you cannot always change people as they tend to resent being changed as they find it controlling. Acting jealous, controlling or possessive can drive people away, and that is the last thing Librans want as Librans love people and hate being alone. You do not mean to be any of these things as they are not typical of you, but you may sometimes act automatically in this fashion or come across as acting this way. This stems from an insecurity within right now about life – things are changing and you cannot always predict where and what changes will happen next, this leads to a control reflex kicking in. However, sometimes the more we try to control any situation, the worse it gets, and this can lead to a self-fulfilling prophesy. The lesson is this, do not compromise yourself to be what others want you to be, be yourself and be true to yourself.

This is somewhat of an uncertain period in your life where you need to learn to let go, to trust the universe and to have faith (in both yourself and the universe). You may experience uncertainty this year from your partner: his/her behavior may be erratic or events in the life of your partner may throw things in your life into question. You need to go with the flow and accept that it is a dynamic situation with opportunities for growth as well as new things to become accustomed to. In both family and marital relationships, you must be more autonomous, independent and assertive – get in touch with exactly what it is you need to live a more full and meaningful life.

Events this year are often unexpected and unplanned for, and your ability to adapt and to be resourceful will be tested. You will also discover many latent talents and abilities you have, which may not have come to the fore had these events not unfolded. The fabric and set up of your life are changing, and you have a chance to mold the future for better. Accept the inner restlessness within you and the call for changes. Get rid of the responsibilities that are holding you back. Purge from your life the things that limit your independence and self-expression. While Librans crave balance and order, this is a year to embrace chaos and be more in touch with the wilder side of you – there is more to life, and there is more to you ... so go after what you are passionate about. The more you suppress the need in you for a change of direction, the more you will attract disruption from others and expose yourself to random events – reflect on where and why you are discontented, and work to make changes. I don't suggest radical changes that shock everyone around you, but do be assertive about the changes and let everyone know you mean business. Listen to your heart and deepest emotions and do not make wrong decisions based on ego considerations.

This is also a time that is deeply transformative on a psychological level, and you have the chance to kick negative mindsets and negative thought patterns out of your mind for good. This is an excellent year to seek counselling or to seek resolution on a matter that has troubled you for years. End the chapters of your life that no longer work for you.

2015 is an exciting time that is neither humdrum nor routine; there is electricity in the air and restlessness in your soul. Seize the energy of the planets to awaken yourself to a more honest self-expression and to living your life on your own terms, true to your unique values and along the path of your destiny. Take a stand and do not shy away from setting yourself apart from the crowd. Sometimes a confusing, bewildering time, but more than that, it's an exhilarating time, which can recharge your with excitement about your life again.

LIFE

Taking stock of finances this month is important for finances sake, it should not lead you to equate yourself with what you earn. We make money; we are not made of money. Money should not define our self-worth.

This is a month of dealing with practical things and getting your head back into work after the holidays. It is best to take the month as it comes and not plan anything too challenging or mentally draining as *slow and steady* rather than *all guns blazing* is the key phrase.

You should not look to others or to the world for some sort of validation as it may not be forthcoming, or it may not even be helpful. At the end of the day, it is what you think about you which counts, it is your life to live and as the song goes, "one life and there's no return and no deposit." Do not compare yourself to others or make choices you hope will please others. Remember that pleasing others is never a guarantee of acceptance and love; pleasing yourself is a guarantee of some satisfaction. Do not give others what they do not want.

Look within for support and encouragement – be your own cheerleader and take that confidence and positivity into your workplace and relationships.

It is very important for you to see value is what you do and how you spend your time – that may mean monetary value or a spiritual/moral value. This month, you may begin to reconsider seriously how you spend your time versus the financial or emotional payback you get – it is time to cut out things that provide no financial or emotional payback.

LOVE

Events to do with children can set a spoke in the wheels of your romantic life – babysitters canceling last minute, children's parties and sleepovers. In fact, family life is very hectic and unpredictable, and romantic moments alone are hard to come by.

Even if you do not have kiddies of your own, a family member asking you to babysit may also result in some hassle.

Intellectual stimulation and debate is key in relationships right now; relationships where there is good conversation will thrive while those where you tend only to talk about chores and mundane matters will suffer both in the bedroom and emotionally. Get the meaningful conversations going again; you do not have to talk about delicate issues, as long as you talk and have banter. Reintroducing fun, witty conversation to the relationship is vital to its heath. Life can be exhausting, and it's too easy to become fixated on the iPhone or Twitter; when we get home from work, conversation can be sacrificed for a quiet wine and a soap opera on the telly. Have an evening out, or get around the kitchen table for a hearty meal accompanied by giving each other your undivided, undiluted attention. Talk about politics sport, current affairs, the neighbors, mutual friends, etc. as long as you re-engage mentally. Play games together i.e. chess, cards, bridge, etc. and rediscover some good old-fashioned ways to spend a cozy, evening – even if the kids are driving you bonkers.

Single Librans are after your mind – yes, in love they will seek partners who can educate, enthrall and entertain them. It is not simply affection you are after; you want someone you admire and respect intellectually – new romances without that element will fail.

CAREER

With Mercury retrograde after the 22nd of the month, it is best to tie up all deals involving: royalties; share transactions; stock market deals; sports related contracts and arts related deals before that time. If you work in law, issues to do with children, custody, and intellectual property rights can become more complicated after the 22nd.

It's not a good month to gamble or take risks, stick to what you know. In any career, be very careful not to plagiarize and make sure that you have the rights to whatever images you use on your advertising, blogs, Facebook pages, etc. Copy write issues may arise this month, so be safe and check out any legal issues before you publish to the web or in traditional media.

In art careers, it can be a case of back to the drawing board – ideas need to be refined and modified to be successful. Do not cut corners, work through all ideas thoroughly to test their efficacy.

Finances are in focus at your work – keep receipts and update filing systems to make sure that all your invoices and financial paperwork can be easily tracked and traced. In your job, be more organized and do not leave matters that should be dealt with until the last minute. Check all bank statements to see that cheques have cleared and that invoices and payments are received. Chase up everything and do not assume the post office or bank will get it right.

LIFE

This is set to be a very hectic month, and you will be required to think fast, make spur of the moment decisions and mentally juggle three different things at once. Get everything written down and keep a diary to make sure you do what you need to do in time, and keep track of what you have done.

This is a time of very good ideas, and so be sure to keep a record of these ideas when they hit you so that they do not get lost in the general hubbub of life.

It is a month of extensive movement – local travel for work and travel for extended family engagements. Planes, trains and automobiles are the stories of February, but it is stimulating and exhilarating if not nerve-wracking at times.

You are very good at problem solving this month even where the problems are complex and you seem to be the one who is not afraid to say what others steer clear of. You have the ability to see what is real and what is false and to expose the truth for the better of everyone – this may not make you popular but it must be done. Your judgment is sharp and you are able to give some of the best advise going – even if it is not what people want to hear…is good advice ever what we want to hear???

This is a very good month for communicating with people – as long as you take your time and don't rush everything. The sheer volume of communications means that you cannot spend as much time with every individual you deal with in work or socially as you would like – remember not to be abrupt or to appear to brush people off.

LOVE

Librans are the initiators in love this month – whether it be sex, social activities, nights out or affection, you will be the one to get you both motivated and to get romance going. You are also proactive in settling arguments and issues between you in order to get back to normal as fast as possible. There will be some arguments this month as you are strong-willed in love, but these will be settled fast without lingering hostility.

Full of fun and energy, you are very expressive and tactile – you want to show your love with words, actions and intimate affection. Quality intimacy with cuddles and pillow talk is very important to you – you want to really feel the love, and the more time your partner is willing to spend giving you pleasure in both the bedroom and beyond, the better things will be. You are certainly in a giving mode and will not hold back. You will also want to initiate activities which bring you both together and which you can enjoy together. It won't just be evenings out; you will want to encourage working out together, sporting events or creative events that you can do together.

Single Librans are also pro-active in love and will be quick to use Valentine's Day to surprise or make a move on someone.

Both single and committed Libra will be all set to add spontaneity and excitement to their love lives as you are vivacious– what a great way to spend February.

CAREER

There will be struggles with your adversaries, and you will have to be creative to keep one step ahead of them. Do not underestimate those you negotiate or deal with commercially, they have tricks up their sleeves and can be tricky to handle.

You may experience extra stress with regard to any client, customer or supplier you are in dispute with – get legal advice early.

Relationships with colleagues are generally good, but there may be rivalries that you are not aware of, but which are affecting your team – try and take this into consideration.

You will have many original ideas on how to increase your profit or how to introduce more services or products which can enhance sales. You are very money-minded right now and may look to ask for a promotion or to seek further training in order to secure a promotion.

There can be profits to be made in the areas of psychology, exploration (or investment) in oil/mineral companies, medical research, geology or private investigation. A good month for detectives or those in police work. Those doing research degrees can be very productive and may get extensively published.

LIFE

The focus this month is very much on health. If you are looking to start a new diet or health diet to improve your overall well-being and fitness, anything you start now can be very successful, and you will stick to it.

Look for local Zumba, Yoga or exercise classes or join a weight loss group – this is a great way to be social and increase your motivation and staying power. Quit smoking or quit sugar, but whatever you do, think more about your diet and your lifestyle and switch bad habits to more healthy habits – a habit either good or bad is hard to break, so start good habits and improve your long terms health. If you have been unwell, this can be a turning point when trying a new treatment can help you immensely. Remember to take a holistic approach to health: mental attitudes and knowing how to switch off from stress can be just as helpful as a good diet. Support your mental health and reduce stress by supplementing with vitamin B complex, calcium, magnesium and zinc. Get more fresh air and take moderate exercise.

Librans are known for their sweet tooth – too much sugar depletes minerals and vitamins and adds to stress, so do your best to reduce the sugar habit.

Pets and animals may play an important role in your life, and you may get a new puppy or kitten or a rescue dog/cat.

LOVE

A very grounded time in relationships, where you can calmly look at your needs and decide how they can be better fulfilled within the partnership. You may shun other social activities and friends to spend quiet time alone with your partner.

Relationships will take on a realistic, mature feel where things can be discussed rationally, and where you can work as a team, contributing equally. It is a very good time to broach joint finances and debate how to curb expenses or invest in your home. A good time for joint decisions about children, money, the home, the in-laws, etc.

Librans will look to cement new relationships and take them to the next level. You may decide to move in together or get engaged. Any decision you take relationship-wise right now will be a well-considered and reasonable one – not a knee jerk reaction to something trivial.

A good time for mixing business with pleasure – business associates you meet may have romantic potential.

CAREER

Look at ways to improve your productivity at work by either making the environment safer, organized, clean, etc. – get your employer to take your rights at work more seriously and to make the workplace fit for purpose. Try and engage with colleagues and participate with them socially to ensure that you bond and can thus have better working relationships.

It is also time to ask yourself seriously if your work situation is having a detrimental effect on your psychology and, thereby, your health. If you do decide that your work is having a negative impact on you, it's time to take action. Look for a new job with a more supportive and positive work environment, or look at how you can (perhaps with others) revolutionize the way you work so that you all work better together – this can benefit your employer as well, so he/she should be willing to help you achieve this. Know your legal rights at work, and make sure they are respected.

If you work for yourself, reduce your stress by looking at how outsourcing and delegating can maybe reduce your load. Perhaps you can employ a temp or use an online service to take care of day-to-day activities that take up your time and are not especially difficult to get someone else to do.

Many Librans may have an opportunity to move up within their company or move to a different department.

LIFE

A burst of pro-active positive energy that will inspire you to initiate changes and get cracking on ideas. Not much will get you down this month, and when something goes wrong, you will bounce back with more determination.

A cheerful, bubbly persona will also help you to make new contacts in whatever new venture you choose to pursue. You are very outgoing and are giving the impression to others of someone who can make things happen. Events will help boost your confidence, and you are likely to attract people who can be of help to you in the new plans you are making. This is a month of good karma, and where the power of attraction can be used much to your advantage. Don't let the good vibes lull you into a feeling of complacency, things will come to you if you take chances and take control of your life, they will not just fall into your lap with no effort.

You are rather adventurous this month and may try new sports or activities or perhaps weekends away to places that challenge and educate you. You want to stretch yourself this spring, both physically and mentally, which is great, but don't overdo it.

LOVE

You are feeling healthy and vibrant this month and have far more energy than usual, and that bodes well for your love life as you have more zest for both sex and giving your partner more moral and practical support. If your partner has been feeling low, this is the month when you can jolt him/her out of the blues and give him/her some valuable advice and encouragement. In fact, you are not in short supply of advice to give right now, and you may put your money where your mouth is by using your extra energy to help out in a practical way too. Your libido is high, and you are always up for new sexual activities and games.

Single Libra will as with last month be the one to initiate new relationships: you will be attracted to bold, adventurous types who like risk and who seem carefree. What you should not do is pretend to be what you are not just to attract the guy/girl you have set your heart on, i.e. don't pretend you love rock climbing if you have never been near a cliff before and hate heights. Do not be inclined to exaggerate to gain the approval of a prospective lover – let them love you for who you are.

CAREER

Libra are not always overtly competitive; you prefer co-operation rather than competition, but this month you are very competitive and eager to beat off competition. You are able to instill teams and workmates will energy and enthusiasm.

Librans who teach or coach can be especially effective in competitions or in helping others to achieve. It is a good month to take a chance on doing something differently as it may pay off in a big way.

If you work in partnership, this can be a difficult month with disagreements over finances and resources – it will take time to find a solution to accommodate you both, and it may get heated.

Be very clear on all tax issues and ask for advice sooner rather than later.

If you are applying for a loan, you must be persistent, forceful and willing to put a lot of energy into the process as there may be some hoops to go through. You must show that you are well organized.

LIFE

This is a month of verbal and mental battles; you will have to fight hard to win acceptance for your ideas and plans, convincing people will not be easy. Your patience is at a premium this month, and your fuse is short, especially mid-month. You will tend to blow up and lose your temper quite quickly. You may argue with colleagues or siblings. You are very irritable, and you have reason to be; little things going wrong will be a real irritation, and it is a frustrating time.

It is worth remembering that more haste is less speed, and you may actually achieve more by backing off and leaving something and rather picking it up at a later stage when you can deal with it more calmly. With people, just leave them be, the argument that seems so important at the time is not actually that vital and is best walked away from. If they will not accept your point of view, leave it, they may come round to your way of thinking later, and pressuring them could actually alienate them.

Your energy is high right now, and you are mentally alert, but it can be very hard to channel that energy in constructive ways. This is a good month for standing up for yourself, for tackling physical chores and for doing lots of little jobs rather than one long drawn out one. If you can plan ahead, make sure that you do not schedule something that needs concentration and sustained effort for May. If you need to do something in a rush, last minute, then maybe the energies this month are just right for that – but do not cut too many corners!

This can be an excellent month for students cramming for exams.

LOVE

Single Libra may experience intense sexual attraction to someone new, which results in a rather hectic romance. This romance can be rather compulsive, but can also be highly disruptive to your life and can start and end suddenly. Even if this relationship is brief, it can be very revealing, and you may find that you can talk about matters that are very sensitive to you with this person. Being able to share your deepest feelings with this special someone will feel very good, and even if you don't hit it off long term, you can still be friends.

Sudden explosions can erupt in marriages, and you will both take this opportunity to get things off your chest. Arguments are rather heated, and anything that has been brewing below the surface will come to light quite dramatically. You may both accuse each other of acting in a manner that is overbearing and possessive. This is a good opportunity to redefine the relationship and set some new boundaries. The argument will clear the air, and it is perhaps a good thing for you both to acknowledge that you each need some more space right now and some more respect for the emotions that you may both be going through. In some cases, you may storm out and spend a few nights at a friend or Mom. This little relationship drama is actually quite cleansing in nature, and you will appreciate each other far more afterwards.

Things will calm down towards the end of the month, and the sex should be very good then.

CAREER

Those you work with may find you rather snappy and irritable this month. You have little patience with others, and this is not a great month for teachers, lawyers, instructors or anyone who has to explain detailed concepts to others, as you are simply not focused and may omit details. If you drive for a living, be extra careful this month and leave more time on all journeys. Likewise, business trips may be beset with delays and aggravations, and may not achieve everything you hoped for. The best way to deal with the month is to get everything organized at the start of May, and so if you are rushed and stressed as the month wears on, you can fall back on the work you did early on.

Although you are likely to have many good plans and ideas this month, a scattering of energy and a struggle to get organized due to factors in the outside world, which may be disruptive, and factors to do with legal and language matters will hamper progress.

You will also have to make sure assertiveness does not become aggression in the way in which you deal with situations. This is a very good month for those who work in newsrooms, journalism and fast-paced working environments, where quick thinking is the order of the day

A frustrating and busy month, but you will look back and be pleased with what you achieved, all considered.

LIFE

After all the toil and trouble of last month, you are feeling rather relaxed and chilled. You are in the mood for socializing, good food, and good wine.

This is not a great month to tackle anything technical; so do not try DIY or assembling anything from IKEA ☺

This is certainly an opportune time for reading, artistic hobbies or going away somewhere quiet by the sea or a lake. You are in the mood for tranquility and to pamper yourself and also to have a chance to escape mentally and think. I often think that as adults we do not have enough time to THINK; yes, we constantly worry and obsess about work and chores and what we have to do next, but the joy of daydreaming and allowing ourselves to think of something fanciful or of nothing in particular can be lost. Escape in good books, movies or music thins the month and allows the arts to awaken your soul to the beauty of life beyond the madding crowd.

This month, helping a friend or family member who is in need can give you a real sense of pleasure and purpose. So often, we feel very alone in this life, as if it's each man for himself, period! However, this month your interaction with others will remind you of the intrinsic connection we all have and the joy one can have through experiencing that.

Allergies can affect you, and so be careful of what you eat and drink – check the ingredients.

LOVE

A much smoother month love-wise; you are feeling romantic and dreamy. It would be ideal if your partner treated you to a romantic dinner somewhere special or a surprise trip to the theatre.

The one danger is carelessness about communications – be sure what you say is understood properly, as misunderstandings can derail the romance. Say things clearly and don't assume anything, get it straight.

Single Librans may have a surprise romantic communication or a mystery admirer who sends flowers or a message. Who in your circle fancies you but is afraid to make the first move? That is the question.

A good month for new and established relationships, whether you party or just veg out on the couch – it's fun and enjoyable.

CAREER

A very good month for those who work in creative careers – you have time to be imaginative and not too many deadlines (like last month). The one danger being that although you are creative, you can struggle with practical issues to do with your projects.

A particularly successful month for those who work in alternate fields, homeopathy, natural medicine or health food – you are able to help people and successfully communicate the benefits of your field of medicine or health, generating interest and new clients. A very good month to write about or hold a seminar on holistic health and well-being.

A close bond can be formed with colleagues this month with a keen sense of community developing in your workplace. However, if there are serious underlying issues and dissatisfaction within your place of work: mistrust, deviousness and even dishonesty can be a problem, and so do beware of these issues intensifying this month.

Be careful of people who work with you that freeload or are not responsible due to emotional issues they are going through this month.

LIFE

A good time for studies, creative and spiritual pursuits – it is a time of a broad and open-minded search for answers. You are looking to expand your understanding of the universe and yourself, and you may choose to do that via science or alternate means.

This is a time when you can expand your contacts and possibly meet influential people who can help advance your career and open doors for you.

There can be opportunities to further your learning, especially in legal fields, where you may specialize in a field in order to help you in both your career and in your political and social endeavors. You are seeking to use knowledge as leverage and as a way to advance your aims.

Travel internationally is likely, especially if it involves learning about another culture, political system or religion.

LOVE

You are feeling a little shy and restrained in love this month – you need reassurance right now, and that needs to be verbal and emotional reassurance. You may take a small criticism or rebuff more seriously than usual as you are feeling touchy and a little sensitive. If you do not get the tenderness and understanding you crave, you may become a little withdrawn. It's best to let your partner know that you need a little TLC, rather than sulking or playing a martyr.

It may be that you are required to make a sacrifice for the one you love this month – it may be giving up something you really want to do or forgoing something you needed yourself, but you will be tested in how you react to having to make this sacrifice. If love is strong it should be easy, but if you resent making this sacrifice then maybe you do not care as much for this person as you thought, or it may reflect buried resentments which are usually hidden from sight. You may feel like, "Why should I forego what I want when she/he would not do that for me?" It could be a good barometer for how the relationship is really going deep down.

It is a month when what goes on beneath the surface in relationships, i.e. the subtle power plays, the balance of power, and the give and take are unearthed.

CAREER

Your ambition is stimulated this month, and you will strive to achieve and to excel – it is important for you to be seen to have authority and taking the back seat or working behind the scenes will not be very fulfilling. You may lock horns with your manager or boss as you will have a clear idea about how you think something should be done – use your Libran persuasive skills to bring him/her around to your way of thinking and be patient, do not go ahead and do your own thing as you know how authority figures hate being upstaged.

You have quite a bit of energy and drive to put towards your career goals this month, and so it is worth ramping up the old CV and sending it out or perhaps checking out recruitment agencies for positions which are more in line with your ambitions. Ask yourself: is there a future for me in this company? If no, now is a good time to look elsewhere.

In self-employment, this is a good month to increase your visibility and public profile – look at ways to get your name known, and do not underestimate the power of word of mouth. Reputation management is very important – ask you clients to write reviews online, and make sure you are listed everywhere you can be on the web.

LIFE

Your powers of perception are sharp, and your judgment is good this month. You can take a broad view, which will aid you in making informed and wise decisions. You are feeling quietly confident this month and are communicating in a way that expresses this confidence and optimism, which means you can make a very good impression on people. A really good month to work in groups as you are seen to be inclusive, and it is easier to get everyone on board with your ideas.

This month it is as if the wind is in your sails and lady luck is smiling on you – you feel pretty good and will find opportunities for both pleasure and financial gain. A very good time to formulate and act on goals.

A good month to smooth over difficulties and offer up an olive branch – you are magnanimous and eager to move on in situations where there has been ill feeling. You have a fair degree of foresight right now, and that is very useful in giving loved one's advice – whether they ask for it or not.

You are feeling brave right now, and that can extend to tackling people or tasks which you would normally avoid, it can also mean facing up to things about yourself that you are often in denial about – dealing with the issues can even lead to a great surge of confidence!

LOVE

Friendship is very important to you in your marriage, and you value the time you spend with your partner doing and enjoying things together. Wherever you are, you must make time to have fun as a couple, not as parents or as hardworking tax payers, you need time to leave your cares at home, even if only for a few hours and have a good laugh and a good chat together.

Relationships can be up and down this month as emotionally you are in flux – you should not read too much into this, your needs are not constant, and you will have to ask your loved one to be patient. One moment you want to party, and at other times you prefer to be alone with a book.

Single Librans may blow hot and cold in love, one moment being up for it and the next feeling decidedly disenchanted with the same person you could not stop thinking about five minutes back.

You are fluctuating between one extreme and another in love this month, but what you really do not want is to feel controlled and bossed around – a boy/girlfriend or husband/wife who respects your moods and allows you space this month will be greatly appreciated.

CAREER

An excellent time for negotiation, group discussions and contractual negotiations. Legal matters are often resolved at this time.

If you have a company expense account be very careful not to overspend on it as the temptation this month is to spend too much money on business entertaining, client benefits and business lunches. You should review the amount you budget for advertising carefully, client hospitality, promotions etc. and ask yourself if this money brings in more than it costs. Look for more effective ways of advertising and analyze your ROI from all your marketing expenses.

In employment, do be careful of becoming over familiar with colleagues of the opposite sex as they may become a problem that could affect your work life, especially if teamwork is important in your office.

You are very energetic at work and eager for leadership roles and experience in different departments or capacities, this can be a great month to impress the boss or expand your experience for CV purposes; on the downside, know your limits and do not bite off more than you can chew to impress colleagues as it may not work out to your advantage.

LIFE

Expect the unexpected – this can be a hectic and surprising month for you. You are set to be very busy, and things will not always run according to plan. You will be having extensive and almost frenzied communications with people and must be sure that everything is understood clearly as misunderstandings are possible.

Routine is NOT the byword for September, anything but. You will have to be inventive and adaptable in the way you handle events. Events to do with extended family or siblings may also demand your attention and will arise out of the blue.

If you have been ignoring something and hoping that it would go away, now is the time it will jump out at you like a Jack in the Box – so act now to avoid difficulties when this happens.

Events politically and economically that are dynamic can also have a direct impact on your life.

If you have children, they can really test you right now in terms of 'freedom' issues, and there can be many generation problems where you will have to acknowledge that things have changed so much that your own standards, morals and principles will have to bend.

Events this month will test your thinking: both your imagination and your preconceived ideas about the world. Your thinking must adapt and fast.

Mental exhaustion due to stress is an issue this month, and so plan ahead and build in extra time for this month so that you are not stretched, and you can have some time to chill out and take a mental breather.

Eating fast junk food is a problem this month – watch your sugar and fat intake as these add to stress levels. Avoid drugs and legal or illegal highs.

LOVE

Relationships can take the strain this month, and sudden arguments are possible. Try as hard as you can not to work at cross purposes – if you talk about how to handle the things that come up beforehand and agree who does what, it can be far better than dealing with things ad hoc. Communicate well with each other, and keep each other posted. Have a clear plan you both agree on.

You may be separated from your partner due to work: one of you may need to travel to work elsewhere. You may find this challenging to adjust to on many levels.

Librans are big flirts this month, and single Librans are very enthusiastic socially and romantically; you are likely to start a new relationship very quickly, although it may not live up to your high expectations. You are pretty insatiable right now in terms of your craving of excitement and romance, be careful not to act in haste and get yourself into a tricky situation. Have fun by all means, but do not take risks and remember that all that glitters is not gold in terms of love.

CAREER

Keep an eye on economic and political events as they may impact directly on your business or career – there can be opportunities if you act fast.

If you work in partnership, sudden events to do with that person or people can have an impact on the way you work and may result in disruption and you having to undertake new job descriptions.

Librans are not usually techno-minded, in fact, Libra are often techno phoebes – but this month you need to get to grips with technical innovations, i.e. new computer programs, new devices, new systems, etc. There may be glitches in new software that you have installed on your website, and you might have to become an expert whether you like it or not in order to keep things going.

If you are off work due to having a baby, you may now be itching to get back into work or back to the work you were doing.

Changes in your workplace may be the catalyst for you to quit a job you don't like and seek something new and more inspiring.

LIFE

The time is now right for critical decisions and for bringing things that have been problematic or tapering off to a close. Look to concluding any project or activity in your life that is no longer providing value for time or money.

Do it now – is the motto for this month.

Balancing the amount of time and energy you spend on yourself versus others is also crucial – you may have been spending too much time on yourself selfishly and now the special people around you have begun to feel neglected, or it may be that you have been people-pleasing to such a degree that you have lost yourself, and you need to claim backspace and time to be you and to redefine your identity.

The emphasis is not on what you have done, but on who you are and how you want to be seen by others. Relationships (both business and personal) and how these contribute to your self-image and confidence will have to be analyzed – it is time to cut contact with those who make you feel negative and bring you down. Put a red ring around the Debbie Downers, the Gary Gossips and the Toxic Tanyas you know and show them the door.

This month ask yourself what you are waiting for – we are always waiting for the right time and often there is not 'right time' we must just take the chance and do it.

LOVE

You are inclined to bring up matters that you have been going over in your head for some time this month. It is a great time to talk things out – you will feel like you have the words to express what you have wanted to say for a while, but which you felt unable to. You are also able to take on board criticism from your partner and handle this in a logical way without being hurt. It can be a great time to talk about where relationships are going – will you move in together, will you get married, will you have another child, should you spend time differently, ways in which you can both contribute more to helping things work?

Relationships are dynamic, and yet all too often we expect them to be routine and can get insecure when things change; this month, you should talk about how the relationship can change for the better for both of you, this will, of course, also mean your sex life. Making assumptions in relationships often causes problems, and this is the time to iron out any incorrect assumptions or preconceptions you may be carrying about that are hurting communication and harmony. A good time to embark on marriage counselling if that is what is needed.

Single Librans will be unwilling to commit this month – you are not short of admirers, but you are not settling for second best, and you need to be 100% sure. You are not wanting to waste time on romances that are going nowhere.

CAREER

A very good time for all careers involving communications. You are very verbal and eloquent right now, especially when you talk about subjects close to your heart.

An excellent time for dealing with facts, figures, words and ideas which bodes well for accountants, bankers, teachers, journalists, copywriters and promoters. However, since most jobs or business ventures involve using words or figures to some degree, this month gives a boost to every Libran's confidence when using these. You may be a masseuse placing an ad in the paper and you find you are very good at coming up with an eye-catching slogan for your business, you may be a creative person who suddenly finds the financial side of your business easier to grasp and more interesting. In whatever business or line of work you are in, be bold with words and numbers: expand your knowledge of basic accounting and improve your vocabulary.

An excellent month for negotiation and deal making – you are very persuasive and diplomatic. A good time for lawyers, arbitrators and politicians.

LIFE

Careful and systematic about what you do, you are perfectionistic and precise this month and are leaving nothing to chance. You are very motivated and committed to concrete results this month; you will ignore distractions and work tirelessly to achieve something you have set as a goal. You must be careful not to become so bogged down in the detail that you miss the bigger picture.

You have a very real sense of personal responsibility this month – you have also set your standards very high and will not be tolerant of time wasters and people about you who are not pulling their weight. This is not a month when you will suffer fools gladly, and your criticisms can even be quite harsh at times – although fair. Librans are known for being tough but fair, and that is your motto this month. You are also just as critical of yourself, but you must learn to take a step back this month as you could lose sight of the wood for the trees, and that may be counterproductive. Do not work in isolation and remain open to outside ideas.

It is also a month of assessing where you are in terms of the life changes you have been working on – how are things going, and do you need to think more about where exactly you are headed to on this adventure we call life? Life is an adventure after all, your unique adventure, and so never stop thinking, growing, striving and never accepting second best.

LOVE

November is a somewhat serious time in relationships – commitment, dedication, stability and thoughtfulness are what you are looking for and needing. If your partner is behaving frivolously, irresponsibly or childishly, you will not be happy with them.

It's one of those overworked, underappreciated months, and you are wondering if he/she has already forgotten everything you spoke about last month? You may be in a slightly glass is half empty frame of mind when it comes to relationships – your own tiredness, sensitivity and negativity may be leading you to make too much of something that is in reality small. Maybe what you need is a glass of wine and a good party after all?

You really need to relax more in relationships and not take yourself or anything else too seriously this month. The more you cool off, the more he/she will back away, and then you will end up feeling unloved, and it becomes a self-perpetuating cycle. If your relationship is basically sound, you should not overreact to anything that happens this month. If you are feeling that the relationship is actually one of the big things that is holding you back in life or causing you emotional anguish, then perhaps this is the time to start looking at options going forward quite seriously – look to the new year and what your first steps can be to either get the relationship back on track or call it quits.

Librans in newer relationships may decide that the new guy/gal is just not worth it. This is a month when long distance relationships can go through an especially hard time; it is also a month when society/your community may frown on your relationship, i.e. relationships with very large age gaps, cross-cultural relationships, alternate relationships, etc. Remember it's what makes you happy that counts – "never give up on a good thing, remember what makes you happy, if love is what you got, you got the lot," as George Benson sung.

CAREER

You are very result driven this month and are a bit of a workaholic. You are also willing to do those jobs no one else wants to do. You are happy for the buck to stop with you and will take on responsibility as you have a can-do attitude and, what's more, you want to do it. You are in a 'if you want a job done properly do it yourself' mode – it is not that others cannot do it properly, it's that you have a very specific idea about how you want it done and so it is easier for you to do it yourself than explain every detail.

In your business, you may in-source – is that the right word for the opposite of outsourcing? Not sure there is even an opposite to outsource? Let's go with in-source. You may choose to do something yourself that you used to outsource as it may be faster and cheaper, i.e. new accounting software may make it possible for you to keep your own books, new graphic design software may enable you to do your own creative designs and marketing.

A highly productive month, not one of much travel or interaction with others – it's more about detail work, paperwork, office work, admin, etc.

Avoid new financial investment or taking loans – keep it simple financially this month.

LIFE

Have faith in your own visions, beliefs and goals and stick to them. Be your own cheerleader and do not wait for approval nor support from others, go with your gut and go for it. Live your own truth and don't be challenged or coerced into conforming. 2015 has been all about your life path and rediscovering your power, but the work is not done yet. Live according to your own truth and remember that while 'following your dreams' is much talked about on X-factor and is not always practical, we all have many dreams and not all of them are impossible – in fact most are attainable to some degree, and it is always good to feel that they are being pursued in some way and not buried and forgotten.

Librans are very goal-orientated, and so this is a great time to set goals to work towards next year – these can be fitness, financial, travel goals or anything at all that matters to you. Write lists and draw up timetables about when and where you plan to make steps towards these goals.

LOVE

You are inspired to do something very different this December – you are decidedly bored with the usual routine celebrations, and you want to spice it up. Perhaps a last minute trip somewhere or a Christmas in the warmth rather than back home with the traditional snow. You are also in the mood for surprises this Christmas; you want to add spontaneity to your love life, as well.

Novelty is just what your relationship needs – get away from the routine, and rediscover who you both are and why being together is so great.

I don't think Librans will have much patience for in-laws this year, so this is another reason why having a Christmas away somewhere could work well for you.

You are very energetic and enthusiastic, and this bodes well for your sex life – but don't just do it the usual way, be inventive, get some erotic books and some saucy undies and be original.

Single Librans are very social and pro-active in love – you may attend speed dating events, double dates, blind dates etc., anything that offers excitement. You are more interested in experimenting with new dating methods and new types of partner than anything committed right now.

CAREER

The first part of December is very busy and will be great for sales, international trade and especially consumer goods – so a good December for your business. It is a lucrative and financially prosperous month for Libra.

You will have to be very decisive and provide strong leadership in early December as the pace is very quick, and there is no time to mull things over. Do not take risks or allow a moment of rashness to threaten good work you have done – Librans are very fired up this month, and this can lead to outbursts that are uncharacteristic. Count to 10 OK.

Things will calm down later in the month, and there will be plenty of time to get ready for the holiday and all the celebrations.

Now I am not a weatherman, but take into account that extreme weather (be it snow in the US, heat in Australia, rain in the UK) may affect your business this December so make sure deliveries go out early, and that you have relevant insurance cover. If you work in a team, do take into account that many workers may not be able to make it in mid-December due to either weather chaos, electricity blackouts or strikes, make sure they can work from home and be flexible. Ensure your computer systems are free of glitches pre-Christmas rush.

The final ten days of December look good – time to put your feet up and give yourself a well-earned pat on the back.

THANK YOU so very much for buying this book! Have a wonderful 2015, all the very best to you.

CPSIA information can be obtained at www.ICGtesting.com
Printed in the USA
LVOW11s1450120115

422492LV00002B/336/P

9 781503 053038